TH

DEV

EA

T

There Devil, Eat That

ERE
IL,
T
HAT

poems by

JONARNO LAWSON

PEDLAR PRESS | Toronto

ACKNOWLEDGEMENTS
The publisher wishes to thank the Canada Council for the Arts and the Ontario Arts Council for their generous support of our publishing program.

LIBRARY AND ARCHIVES CANADA
CATALOGUING IN PUBLICATION

Lawson, JonArno
There, devil, eat that / JonArno Lawson.

Poems.
ISBN 978-1-897141-44-1

I. Title.

PS8573.A93T425 2011 C811'.54
C2011-906046-9

COVER ART *Icarean*, Haydon Chapel, Dorset 1993 and *Snake Skin*, Mearshurst, Surrey 1997. Silver Gelatin Prints by David Ellwand

DESIGN Zab Design & Typography, Toronto

TYPEFACE Adobe Garamond

Printed in Canada

The Canada Council for the Arts since 1957 | Le Conseil des Arts du Canada depuis 1957

ONTARIO ARTS COUNCIL
CONSEIL DES ARTS DE L'ONTARIO
An agency of the Government of Ontario

These poems are dedicated to those I'll never now be able to thank.

Thinking, in the sense in which we usually mean the word, is something that happens between people. If we can manage it by ourselves later in life, it is only because we have previously had someone close by to do it with us.

— Charles Fernyhough, *The Baby in the Mirror: A Child's World from Birth to Three*

Your severed head lies on the floor
I throw it out the open door
your body follows it, and then
puts your head back on again.

— Sophie Freedman-Lawson, *Collected Poems*

If you had to choose between these two sides, which would you choose? The side led by one smart and one stupid person, or the side led by two who were just average?

— Ashey Freedman-Lawson, *Pensées Politiques*

'Nake 'nake! 'Top! Baby 'cared!

— Joseph Freedman-Lawson, *Talking without Esses*

What is the difference between the moments you want to live to see, and the moments you would die for?

— Adnan Ali

"The wind moved and the leaves applauded. The garden hose hissed and slithered. The grass disappeared, and in its place roared a black, black sea."

— Lenore Look, *Alvin Ho*

CONTENTS

There Devil, Eat That

HOW I STARTED TO WRITE WELL

I started to write well
when I stopped trying to write well
I started to write well when I started to notice what was
noticeable but not often noticed —
(it was lucky I noticed I noticed!) —
I started to write well
when I dropped my bucket into the well, and well,
well well.
I started to write well when I stopped stopping to yodel or yell
and now I swell
with pride when I think of how badly I used to write
compared to how I write now! And how!
And now, when I think about it
I started to write well
when I stopped paying attention to what's too dull to mention
and paid more attention to the extra dimension
which you saw through (before you saw it —
I saw it
before I saw through it) —
First learn to hop and then
hop to it
is all I can say
about how to do it
and don't screw it up when you're done — don't undo it
don't do to yourself
what you don't want done to it
do or undo or undo and do it —
you won't know where to stop or to start till you're through it.

TO BEGIN

The breeze along the river reeked of rot
A telephone was ringing in the breeze
A mountain rose to block all second thoughts

Enervated, fingering the keys
longing now to stop
and lie down in the gravel by the road

I thought my head was going to explode —
I fished about to find an empty page
With frigid fingers, fumbling frozen words

Was it their thawing bloody bodies that brought about the awful
buzzing?
I stopped and swatted —
flung an empty core into the wind. Now, to begin…

THE WANDERING ATTENTION OF AMPHIMACHUS DURING A STRATEGY SESSION TOWARD THE END OF THE TROJAN WAR

What was that? Oh, right — of course,
don't neigh inside the Trojan horse…

FORGET ABOUT GETTING

Forget about getting from A to Z
I can't even get from A to B
I can't tell my elbow from my knee
(or my arse from my head, if you prefer Zed)
I'm forgetting.

Forget about getting from 1 to 2
I can't even get from me to you
What was given's been gotten but it's all gone rotten
I'm betting, betting, I'm forgetting.

Forget about getting forgotten again
He'll remember where, she'll remember when
It happened once, you were gone for months
I was aiding and abetting, so upsetting I was fretting,
I was sweating, I was sweating, I'm forgetting.

Forget about getting from morning to night
I can't even get to the dawn's early light
I'm regretting ever getting into anything indebting
All the troubles now besetting me, and nobody is letting me forget them

but

I've forgotten

what

I'm forgetting...

MY LEGS

My legs gave me no pleasure last night
It wasn't their fault
I refused their dog-like entreaties
To enjoy them
To take them for a walk
To use them why not?
They asked
But I ignored them
I made them kneel till they were numb
When they were finally silent I lay down
Loosened the stiff caps off their puckered lips
And slept.

SINK

You're driven by desire
I'm drifting on a whim
You're heading for the centre
I'm clinging to the rim
You keep growing brighter
I keep going dim

You go I stop
You lift I drop
You stare I blink
We're out of sync

And when it's time to dive straight in
You won't need to stop to think
You'll dive in and swim and swim —
I'll slip off the edge and sink.

THE CROWD

In the dark room
unfamiliar and overfull
certain empty outlines lit
up and filled in

with the features of my
wife and the
faces of my
children — friends family

just a few but
most outlines stayed empty
went dark or
disappeared altogether others

filled in briefly
and then vanished
who were
they the

crowd was enormous
and the number
that lit up
was small so small

in the entire
crowd those few
were all that
mattered

I reached and
reached
but never
grasped the rest.

BROTHER AND SISTER: LITTLE NIGHT MOVEMENTS

He murmured her name in his sleep,
she shifted —
her ribs lifted gently
then fell, then lifted.

A BIT OF ME, A BIT OF YOU

A bit of me a bit of you
a bit of the past
and the future too —
we brought you into the world.

We loved you out of the endless night
out of the earth and the passive stones,
we gave you the code for flesh and bones
and we brought you up in the world.

A cornice
you avalanched out of the womb and into a crib in your own
little room,
we tucked you up into photographs (one face at a time under
sheets of glass)
on the edge of the glittering world.

While under the latest crop of stars, you walk to us
and run from us and run to us
and run from us — come back to us now little one
from the edge of the glittering world.

TWO BLUE PAPER EYES

You drew two eyes on a piece of paper
lifelike in their blueness.
You said they would watch me,

tacking them up on the wall
in the place best to watch me from.
Then you went away, and I grew to like the idea

that those eyes really saw everything I did,
and I did everything in front of them
I could think of to shock you, thinking

they were mute, paper eyes — a stupid joke.
But out of an absence
I had not bothered to measure you came back,

approached the horrible eyes
and drew a mouth
that spoke.

TWO SHARED A BREATH

Two blew it into One
and One revived
while Two weakened.

One blew it back into Two and weakened
while Two revived and
that's how the two of them

lived and survived till Two
felt deprived,
and coughed,

and One
took a breath
and ran off.

I LEAN FORWARD

I lean my head forward
to rest.
Suddenly I realize
that I hold in my hands

a live face recumbent
soft and bony
and ugly
as a frog.

PEOPLE HUNTING

When my father was seventeen he took his gun to Germany
and he went people hunting.
Sometimes he'd lie in a tree's dark shade and pull the pin from
a hand grenade (lobbing it inexpertly at no one in particular).

He'd come to collect a German head to mount at home above
his bed. He hunted and hunted and hunted. Over the rolling
Bavarian hills with the zeal that a gun in the hand instills —
how he'd prepared in the endless drills

for blood to come jerking and burping and lapping
for startled faces and frightened shouts
but not for the slaughtering laughter, or the grey-green silence after.

Now looking unhappily at the head
he couldn't quite picture it over his bed
so he kept the head in his head instead

where no one else could see it.
And there it kept looking for Lebensraum
but nobody could free it.

WAR AND PEACE — SPECIAL FEATURE! (WHAT'S OUT — AND WHAT'S IN!)

expLOsiVEs
sLAUGHTER
JeOpardY
disapPEAranCE

THE DEATH OF STEVEN STRATYCHUK, FEB. 26, 1945

Stratychuk was dead
and the tongue in his cheek was dead
and every last thought that had been in his head
was gone now from his head

though all around him
everyone rushed backward
forward upward
downward.

No mother's hand (or agony)
would stand him up again.
Thrown up on a wagon he
was Steven less and less

and not a single word he said
passed down
when silence grabbed him by the mouth
and pulled him underground.

THE HAMILTON BUS — *for Grandma*

She bitched back and forth
across the basement floor
set the oven roaring
in her pre-dawn rage
to forge her tarts.

Her pastry bowl was half a star snatched from a clear June night, cloven,
and emptied of its light. On the smooth, curved surface of
its implosion she worked with her nicked and crooked fingers.
Up above, from the safety of my room
I heard her mentholated croaks

the setting of the timer
and her voice as it joined in with
the mayhem of her organ-playing.
The fury of her ruminations
filled my room with smoke.

I heard her calling graveyards on the phone
shouting out for ghosts
summoning them to listen to her complaints against time
as if each day was a cruel contrivance,
an unwanted gift

designed to deprive her of another grievance.
But finally
somewhere in the east a bus woke
and rolled
toward her underworld.

IF ONLY

If only
we'd also…
if only.

If only
we'd also had.

If we'd had
we would have

we would've had

and we'd have enough now.

Haven't we had enough now?

No…

Haven't we?

No. No

we haven't —
never have had

never will have.
If only we'd had.
If we'd had, we'd have.

We'd've…
oh yes,
yes we would've.

And had we had
we wouldn't have been had
had we had

and if we hadn't,
if only we hadn't.

If only.

TRAVELS — *for Michael Joseph*

i.
Saint-Fargeau-Ponthierry

Next to the canal lock
where we waited
for the night to begin

a beautiful girl arrived in a boat
she had a bicycle, and parents
and they had a table

they quickly set up next to the lock
under an umbrella
where they'd roped themselves

quite near us.
The beautiful girl rode her bike off
through the trees

and came back very soon
with fresh bread, wine, olives, some cheese,
tomatoes and grapes.

The sun came out. Briefly before setting
for a moment by its light I saw that my real life was over there
with them

my real life had nothing to do with you.
But years would pass before I had another chance
to be in such benevolent company —

why, in such close proximity, did I ignore
my natural sympathies
and turn my back on their quiet celebration?

ii.
Sorrento Susie

I almost spent the evening in Sorrento
with a woman from Montepertuso —
I had nothing at all to lose so
I got on her motorbike near Positano —

she said "Buona sera, mi chiamo Susie!"
I said "Non capico Italiano…,"
she said, "Okay! Then I'll meet you someday
at the Bar de Martino."

So she took me to the beach
after a cappuccino —
she said "I want to leave this place,
I've got a brother in New York City."

I said "How can you leave this place
when it's so pazzesco and so pretty?"
She said "I've been here all my life,
and I've got to go."

Then she took me back up the mountain
and I stepped back onto the ground and
she said "Just one cigarette before I go.
There's so much I want to tell you

about yourself, so I'll call you tomorrow."
There's so much about myself
that I don't know,
so I gave her my number.

iii.
Nuns one night in Krakow

Arriving in the Krakow night
we spot a white-clad Novice on the loose
and then two older Sisters hovering

at a window full of shoes.
Another stands before a statue
of her husband — Christ —

with or without reverence?
Hands on her hips — exasperated —
itching for a fight... "Well there you are!"

petite, defiant, petulant — she bunches up a fist at him
and suddenly shouts angrily
"I looked for you all night!"

iv.
305 rue Marie-Anne est

(*or How my past self tried, unsuccessfully, to disown me*)

I know more about him than he thought I'd know.
Looking back, he didn't know much.
He couldn't guess well —
Certainly he didn't know that I'd come someday

Straight to where he hid in the past
Not to disown him
As he disowned me,
But to gather him back.

v.

On Leave, In Love, In London

(*or The Death of The Beastly Belle*)

A grub-gutted oak levered over by a woodpecker
walloped in the top of a blood red double-decker
caving in the skull of a governmental fact-checker —
diabolic hussy from the Office of the Exchequer —
part-time barfly, heartbreaking home-wrecker.

Hard-hearted laughter as a shock-staggered rubber-necker
grips at his head
moaning "Is she dead?"
"Yes that beastly belle from the Office of the Exchequer's dead, dead,
definitely dead!"

AS I HURRY

As I hurry away
The slowness I abandoned continues on
Without me

Even as the first and foremost Me
Rushes down steps, purposeful, gasping
My second-self's slow movement

Abandons itself again
And continues to separate and fragment
Until slowly

I am everywhere
Going nowhere.
A multitude of ever-slower selves

Dragging at everything
A subtle force
Winding the whole world down.

RULE OF THUMB

A simple inspection shows that
when compared to the other fingers
the thumb seems to be missing a joint.

Does it savour this difference,
or loathe its aloneness?

Yes the finger called a thumb
seems to be missing something.
Does its breadth make up for what it lost in length?

Seems to be often pushing
in the opposite direction.

Seems a little short, a little chubby
maybe a bit off track
but also

a little more independent,
a little more cheerful.

The four in a row point this way and that way
but the thumb can agree or not, all on its own.
When the conforming four are afraid and curl over

the comforting thumb protects them,
standing up by their side.

The pinky, the ring, the middle and the pointer go along
like a little band that plays the same old songs
of weakness and wealth, giving-the-finger and false accusations.

While the thumb plucks and grips —
though political, never pokes or points.
Being metacarpully opposable,
it pinches up splits — stops slips.

THE STANDOFF ENDS

The standoff ends
while off in the stands
the oftener heard of the angels demands —
clemency tolerance lenience mercy —

all of the usual angel things,
when a voice less heard
unsteadily
adds —

Wings for a cherub
and dust for a fairy
a beak for the lips
of a broken canary —

It's bound to miscarry
the justice that's done
in the dark,
on the run

With nods
of the head
from the smooth
to the hairy

the culprit,
shorn of his wings
and flung from the top
of a cloud, in pain,

falls down on my tongue
like a drop
of cold
rain.

HOW TO MEET THE KING

If you wish to meet the King
you must think and think and think
of nothing
but the King.

If, for a moment, your thoughts
turn to yourself
don't be surprised if the King decides
to meet with someone else.

If you wish to meet the King
you must think and think and think
of nothing
but the King.

THE BONE-BRINGER

When we left Egypt
I was the bone-bringer —
on my back
I carried our Joseph.

A dozen generations
we left where they were
unmarked. It made no difference,
for Joseph's coat

by then ran round the entire crowd:
We had all been pushed or pushed others into pits,
all sold someone,
or been sold

all accused, or been accused
captured or escaped, all been tempted
by Zulaikha or Joseph,
all foretold the future, or needed our futures told,

we had all played practical jokes, or
fallen prey to them — every one of us had
left the land
of our mothers and fathers

in this never-ending famine.
So we lived by him —
even the unremarked ones —
our lives were his grave,

the bones were his joke —
and we paid a high price for it, for them,
in worthless silver for worthless earth —
for our little piece of Shechem.

THE BABY

He was born
three rivers back
over a road that can't
be bought or fought over

back where my wife went
into the water
and laboured
till he swam free of her —

mustering lungs
to master the air
pulled upwards

by his need
breaking through
out of the wet warmth
the whole world racing away from the point where his head rose.

His small soul-mask
drying
a flexible clay
across the bones
of his face.

Here he is
before the fire
waiting for
his story.
When he hears it

nothing in the world
will seem
more painful
more beautiful
less likely.

AN ACORN

An acorn lies
on the earth
like the head
of a half-dead bull.

When the sun
goads it
one white horn gores
the soil while

the other greens
and breaks for
the sky swinging round at
the sun's red cape.

HERE COMES THE WIND

Here comes the wind
to push your goat over the side of a mountain
to sadden a wall
to darken the sky
to rattle a little tin can —
It comes to toss a tired bird beyond reach of the shore —
here comes the wind
oh friend of the wind
to rid me of your ashes.

SAVED

One gets saved by standers-by
Another by a timely lie
Another one by thinking twice
Another's saved by Jesus Christ —

One hides until the coast is clear
Over his head in a wine-dark beer
Another builds a basement bunker
Another's saved who learns to hunker

Down to do the dirty work.
Another one who goes berserk
Is saved by someone's knowing smirk
And one with an endearing quirk

Is saved by those she was endeared to
Though it seems she also feared to
Save the one who volunteered to
Take her place when death appeared to

Knock her down. The next in line
Was no such bastard
He was saved because he mastered
Some great skill that can't be taught

Another one because she bought
Shares in a downtown parking lot.
It makes no sense, who's saved
Who's not.

And you? You think somebody saved a spot
For you? No spots are left, someone forgot
You needed saving
(maybe you'd been misbehaving?).

You're on your own now.
Stand up stranger —
It's time you turn
To face the danger.

LITTLE MARION

I miss little Marion.
She became a woman
but back when I was a boy
she was a girl

and a good friend.
I remember her
standing up tall
at the back door,

how we both watched silently.
While the others
quarrelled:
our solemnity.

Her prettiness, her goodness,
resolute and solitary.
I met her again, years later.
I see her now and then in supermarkets.

She's friendly.
She is who she is,
she always was —
But

it isn't her,
little her.
It's not little Marion.
It's little Marion I miss.

THERE THERE...

Here was
there back
then back
when here
was there
here there
was horror,
that's why
we're here!
Because it
was there
because of
the horror
that happened
when it
was there,
back then,
well, here
we are,
where they
were when
it was
there. There
there, we'll
be all
right they
weren't all
right — but
that's all
right that's
why we're
here! We'll
be all
right. All
right? Right —
there there.

ANOTHER LOOK

I took it
That old thought of him
I'd kept
And tried it out with words
To have another
Look at him:

He came in,
He'd been outside.
His face was cold
I guess
I didn't touch it
His cheeks were red
His eyes wide-set

Open, wet.
He came I guess
And went
Though in those days
No one cared much
If he came or went.

Much later
It was added to his legend
That no one cared
Much if he came or went
In the days before his name
Was known

Before the many
Who had tried
To put him off
Or leave him out
Tried instead to put him
Into words.

I GOT UP

I got up
I thought a little
I felt a bit
Then I felt a bit better

Wherever I found
Myself
There I was
If I lost track

I glanced in a mirror
There I was again
It seemed to me
To be me

It seemed to me
Unseemly to stop
Being me
It seemed to me...

But enough
Of me,
It's enough really, often enough
Just to be.

ONE SUNDAY IN SASKATOON

I went to a pub called Winston's, and after that walked down to the banks of the big river that runs through the city and is crossed by seven or eight bridges and there met a little group of elderly people who were having a silent vigil at the memorial to soldiers

killed at Vimy Ridge. Part of their vigil (as they explained to me, hastily scribbling on post-it notes, staying true to the silent part of their vigil) was to put post-it notes up on the columns of the memorial remembering those killed in wars, one way or another. They were going to send them to the Prime Minister when it was over.

I was completely taken with the idea. I wrote a post-it note to remember "two Bavarian boys killed by mistake, in anger, by an enraged American soldier in 1945" (a double murder perpetrated by a good friend of my father's), "my great-great uncle William Wright, who tried to start a new life near Swift Current in the early 1900s,

only to be blown to bits in a trench at Ypres, in 1916" — I could feel myself getting carried away — I could think of at least a dozen more. I had been the recipient of a lot of awful stories! But strangely, I felt happy. Then I saw that the sun was setting, and I noticed the trees on the opposite side of the river, covered in dying leaves. I felt tired. Two girls were

having a picnic nearby — they were rustling their paper-covered sandwiches and giggling. And I noticed too, as I left, that the vigil and my overwrought participation in it were being filmed, for some reason, by an elderly Japanese lady. I'd forgotten Hiroshima, and the massacre of the Chonnonton at the bottom of Emerald Street...

I HATE YOU WITH A HATRED THAT IS THRILLING

I hate you with a hatred that is thrilling.
You don't know yet — but you'll know soon enough.
I hate you with a hatred that is killing
the casual the cool and off-the-cuff —
I hate you with a kind of growing love
a hatred with its source somewhere above —
Unsullied by the coarse and earth-born hatreds we all know
or by those heaven-hindered hatreds festering below.
My hatred is a special kind of love
you don't know yet —you'll know it soon enough.

ITEMS LOST IN SPACE

You, me —
the deep blue sea —
twentieth-century ethics with their strangleholds and death-kicks.
Crumpets, teapots, a farmer's failing wheat crops —
inappropriate topics like sexuality
(in the tropics).
Petitioners, commissioners, prisons full of prisoners —
yachters and their daughters sailing international waters.
My prowess, your shyness
(a handsome horseman for her Highness!)
a metronome for a time-machine
a penitence pill, a forgiveness bean.
I saddle up a satellite and paddle out into the night
to search again for your sweet face —
our love, my love,
is lost in space.

LOVE

I love
You. You,
not you.
I love
you too.
No, not
you. You.

THE GREAT HUMAN DIASPORA (1 to 9)

I
on my
own see now
what must have been
clear other times — stars, comet
trails — orbits unfold across dreams, people
collect, passive, orderly — observe horizon melting skyward
tranquil…peaceful…suddenly — enormous nightsky scatters watchers outwards —
wandering separated homegrown multitude, aimlessly ambitious, traverses limitless distances.

ENDER'S LUCK

If at the start
you're stuck:
you mean to blow
instead you suck

or strike a blow
then when it's struck
you stand
but have to duck —

If at the start
you suffer from
a change of heart
stop short

go numb
and fall apart —
misplace your pluck —
then if you're patient

if you're smart
you'll keep going as you are
there's a chance you'll still go far
if you count on ender's luck.

ARRANGING THINGS

I.

On my knees bent down
I have been arranging things
changing things round.
Engaging in long wanderings
marauding and meandering
and randomly abandoning
my reason and my reasoning,
estranging things from other things —

and I have been endangering and finishing off —
quenching and extinguishing —
begetting and contriving — inventing and imagining,
engendering and fashioning —
exchanging things with other things
and then, oh fate,
humility came late,
too late.

II.

A car stops,
the phone rings
I have been arranging things, changing things round.
A bird sings, the wind brings
cloud formations through the sky. My hands go up
surrendering
my gestures never touch or bring,
or do much of anything. Brought down,
brought down,
the clouds pass, my arms sink, the sun withdraws, the sky shrinks.

A baby's cry, high and thin,
thickens on her mother's breast —
gets muffled up by mothering —
then high and thin, breaks free again.

III.

A mother's hands, a father's wrist,
a wristwatch ticking in a fist —
arm in arm and step by step
they stop a moment and forget. Time will tighten,
time will twist
our little ones away from us.
The tires hiss, the silence rings. I have been arranging things
changing things round, while down
below in the harbour
little boats bob on the swells
under a curious upside-down sky
spangled with star-like shells, sailboat poles
and windblown ropes clang like faraway bells
and I am alone to listen,
and I am alone because
I discovered that life had a meaning, a meaning.
But not what the meaning was.
Does anyone? Somebody does.
It must be that somebody does.

ANSWERS AT THE BACK

"I knew the back way there, but not the way back here"
— Norañjo Alsnow, *Canciones de la botella vacía*

You watch my back I'll watch yours
You're back walking out of doors
I'm back crawling on all fours

Pulling backwards on the oars
You back into foreign shores
Around me spins the bedroom floor —
I back into dresser drawers.

You watch out — I've got your back
Keep your eyes on each man-jack
You back out, as I back in — I know you'll be back again.

Watch my back, go back around
You back up and I'll back down
Your back's wings don't make a sound
My goblin-back goes underground

I front your claims, you back my loss —
Don't backtrack now on the cost — my back starts to turn and toss
Your back's back up on the cross.

But that's your shoulder on my sheet
And that's the morning at our feet
Time that slipped away unseen is
Coming back to lie between us.

Our backs are going back and forth
Yours goes south
While mine goes north —

We grumble on, all growls and grunts
Go backwards twice, go forwards once
So much complaining from the front
When it's the back that bears the brunt.

STILL

Only when absolutely still was it beautiful —
movement ugh its ugly
pulse.

But still, how sweet
it was when
still.

THE DANCE

I returned. She was gone. Another couple had taken our
seats. I asked — Where did she go? They said — Off with
a guy, then out for a smoke. She doesn't smoke, I said, but
wondered as I crossed the gym. I felt worried. Outside the

EXIT stood a stoic fellow in a concert t-shirt, smoking. There
was laughter in the bushes. Where is she? I said. He shrugged.
I peeked into the bushes. Peeping Tom! a voice cried. It wasn't
her, obviously. I kept walking. I thought I saw her in the
distance arm in arm

with someone. I started to run, but stopped. I saw myself as
I thought I saw her — from a distance. I was surprised by a
sudden ambivalence. I'd never realized I could care so little,
so little about someone I cared so much about. This was an
unfamiliar burden, or

was it freedom? I couldn't choose, couldn't choose. I went back
to the dance. There she was, waiting. Where did you go? she
asked. I said — Someone told me you'd gone out for a smoke.
You know I don't smoke, she said. She was perplexed. I was
perplexed.

MINDFUL

His mind — once aflame — had slackened in its pacing;
parts of his torso in need of replacing
took all the blame — his heart, his lungs, his liver and his spleen
and other less known organs in between.

Side by side they watch the movie go
disappearing off the giant screen.
The hero and the villain he's been chasing
meet eye to eye at last, and then you know

What you rip you sew (or was it reap?
Allow what you don't know
in through your dreams —
learn while you sleep!)

The hero's at the fall's edge in the current —
the thunder flow careens about
his legs.
The villain's alligator-grinned elation

excites the hero's righteous indignation.
He clamps his jaw (shaped
something like a box)
and in the end it was his jaw that saved him —

a rope fell from above — dropped by his love
(though earlier the villain thought he'd stopped her —
he'd roughly trussed her — but she wriggled free
and daringly, she flew his helicopter to the scene)

The hero sank his teeth
into the twine — and with a kick the villain flew

astonished
through the swirl —
the hero got the girl,
or so it seemed —

but things that seem
are rarely what they seem,
for it was of the villain that she dreamed.

PROBLEMS

"He wouldn't give
 a bowl of milk to the cat."

"Is that what you heard?"
"Something like that —

 he let it go yowling
 at a neighbour's door,

 then lay down crying
 on the cold stone floor."

"What was his problem?"
"He wouldn't say…

 but his wife came home
 and swept him away."

THE BALD MAN'S STORE

The bald man's store
sold a tonic
to help the balding grow new hair — how ironic.

I asked the bald man
if he planned to try it —
he said "Son, I sell it, but I don't buy it."

OF EIGHT WHO RULED

Of eight who ruled
one ruled wisely —
seven had other things to do
six did them badly

five dreamed of more,
slept more rarely woke.
Four wore ties feared spies
rarely spoke.

Three ground their teeth —
to points to gums to nerves then numb —
(how dismally doomed how dreary and dumb)
on the grit of disappointment.

Two couldn't get further
than bitterness over
that first one
who ruled wisely.

ENDANGERED

For a moment the prospect of safety came close —
Danger itself was in danger!
What could be stranger?
I kept very still while it passed, protective of my peril.

RETREAT

Retreat into your head
Rationalizations, justifications
The space in there is infinite, there's no crime that you can't commit —
You might as well be dead.

Retreat into your heart?
The heart won't allow it — however right you are, you're wrong —
Your heart throws you back into the arms of the world,
Where you belong.

KEYS

In agony over the ebony keys
his fingers fell
into a restless sleep

But woke again on the ivories
Then rested again
in a restless heap

Hunting through hundreds of melodies
Hungering through old memories
Humming her voice back out of the deep

His fingers undoing the atrophy
went reaching again for the apogee
There wasn't a hint of apathy:

Her voice somewhere in a summer breeze
Her voice turning white on the frost-covered trees
Her voice at the bottom of star-covered seas

But never conjured approximately
What he found was revealed with such accuracy
that it rose like some beautiful blasphemy

that only the holy could hear.
And the rest were filled with a restlessness — like arrogant
youthful malcontents
they drunkenly boarded a chariot that none had the strength
to steer.

CORK

Your death —
held back all those years
by a small cork

now extracted
allowed light to be decanted
into the space where you had existed.

We sniff it and praise the vintage.
We drink deeply
at the bright empty edges of your death.

GOODBYE LITTLE TOWN

The winter weather warped the wood
The door's stuck open now for good —

The ugly upped their odds
Jumped pushed fell
The beautiful asked the Gods
To scatter the ugly well
And so they entered the landscape
And there they still dwell.

Design yourself a weapon
And choose your clientele
A weapon you alone can use
A weapon that no one can take from you —
Impinge, expel, impale, impel —
Go do the damage you desire
Doubt the truth and douse the fire.

Inhale in hell — exhale, excel!

The door's stuck open now for good
The ice that entered split the wood
No shelter to be had — I told the road to go away
That touched the bottom of my door

I told the road that touched the bottom of my door
To go away!

Banged brushes on the bricks outside
Set clappers off in bells
The smoky clouds of chalk
Formed letters on the walk

To draw the crowd
But dodge the scout
You long to be discovered
(But not found out).

First you're mocked for caution
Then you're mocked for trying
The poor get mocked for living
And the rich are mocked for dying.

And then I squashed her fingers awkwardly in mine
(What a mistake! Or was it?)
I'm not sure why I did — was it the wine?
(I ask because it…)
"Are you all right?" she asked. I said "I'm fine."
(…because it's difficult to credit when you blame it on the wine.)

A flashing grin for him
A fading smile for me
A dog barks out in the street
At a cat who runs through my dream
They grow apart together
They grow together apart.

She offered an orphaned hour
That nobody else had claimed
As if it were a flower
That hadn't yet been named
I have to admit my attraction
(though now I feel ashamed).

We talk about our childhood
The old familiar neighbourhood
And how we longed to wear the rings of Saturn.

And hoped to find some intricate
And unfamiliar pattern

A melody, a molecule, that we'd reveal and weave
Into the edge of every mind.

Whatever we double
We later divide
Whenever there's trouble
We duck and hide.

But here comes the mob
That jabs and jostles
And jumps for a glimpse
Of the twelve apostles
(Really? They jump
For those old fossils?)

But there's more to it, there's more…
The trains still run through the snow and the stubble
And searchers still search for remains in the rubble
And the east wind sank and the East End stank
And the rain came and went
And the snowstorms swirled
And our little town felt like the end of the world.

Goodbye little town, goodbye.
Goodbye to the edge of the dump
To the knife in my back to the fork in the road to the spoon in
    every pot
To the empty plate that broke in my lap (the innocuous slip and
    the casual slap)
To the axe that rests in the stump
Up past the edge of its edge

Like the beautiful face that drove a wedge
Of distraction through my life. To my edge and beyond my
edge…

MAD BAD MAC!

Old MacDonald had a farm, A E I O U
And when she came across a man, this is what she'd do

Slap that awkward farmhand's back —
Attract that hand abaft a shack
Attack and stab —
drag ass-backwards (past vast dark marshlands —
what a slab, man — call a cab? Pant, pant —
catch a nap and grab a snack)
A hack's black drama —
Mad bad Mac!

Old MacDonald had a farm, A E I O U
And when she came across regrets, this is what she'd do

Retch, spew.
Repent, eschew.
Flex the knees then bend the neck —
here's where she keeps her men secreted —
between the reeds where the spent flesh freezes —
where dew-wet trees meet the sweet bee breezes.

Old MacDonald had a farm, A E I O U
And when she came across his will, this is what she'd do

Hiss: "First things first..."
Twist his wrists —
Strip his thick, stiff limbs — kiss his lips,
diminish him.
His implicit gifts still rising within him,
high spirits, instincts, filling him,
writhing, twitching —
his wild living wish will dim,
shrink, thin. Twilight — night — illicit finish!

Old MacDonald had a farm, A E I O U
And when she came across old sorrow, this is what she'd do

Forlorn, comb blossoms of rot from spoon-smooth brow — howl!
(Oh stop now!)
Lost for good, drop down, chop,
blood flows — who knows how long poor fools hold on —
torpor grows.
Follow protocols! How to conform?
Go to town to shops —
opt for cold comforts. Wrong, wrong —
lost for good.

Old MacDonald had a farm, A E I O U
And when she came across rum luck, this is what she'd do

Sulk.
Gulp suds, drugs, burp —
lug unburnt trunk,
push, pull,
tug — bugs buzz —
skull juts up —
ugh! Unjust!
Mud-stuck — cuss!
(Shut up! Shut up!)
Turn upthrust sulfur
sunburnt bum —
crush shrubs
(tumult, rumpus)
Bush-buds burst —

truth runs up,
shrugs,
succumbs.

Old MacDonald had a farm, A E I O U
but when she came across the why? she didn't know what to do.

CHRYSALIS

The first, whom she resembled most
(with whom she was the most engrossed)
Unfortunately overdosed
Metamorphically.

The one whom she resembled second
Faded when the black hand beckoned
Poison in the blood she reckoned,
Metaphorically.

The one whom she delivered third
Whose little cry was so absurd
Why couldn't she, at least, be cured?
But it was not to be.

The chrysalis needs its cremaster —
silk buttons hold it fast.
It liquefies itself,
but this disaster
sets it free.

It sets aside its past,
persisting metaphysically.

TWO WALTZING

for Amy

We held ourselves in
Till the end of the day,
Then got popped through the rails at an evening soirée —

Now we're two waltzing corks
That dance on the ocean waves
Freed from the bottlenecks holding us tight
We flew through the air and fell well out of sight

We're just two waltzing corks
Untroubled at ease and carefree
Two stars bobbing over a bottomless night
And when the ship's gone, love, we'll still be all right

Nothing can sink us and no one can think we're remiss —
Our job's done, now we've left the abyss
For others to bottle and seal with a kiss
Just like two waltzing corks.

ODE TO LIGHT

KEEP ME IN THE DARK

AND SHADOWS WILL DEFEAT ME

HOLD ME TO THE LIGHT

THE SHADOWS WILL COMPLETE ME

ƎHT M ⅃ H

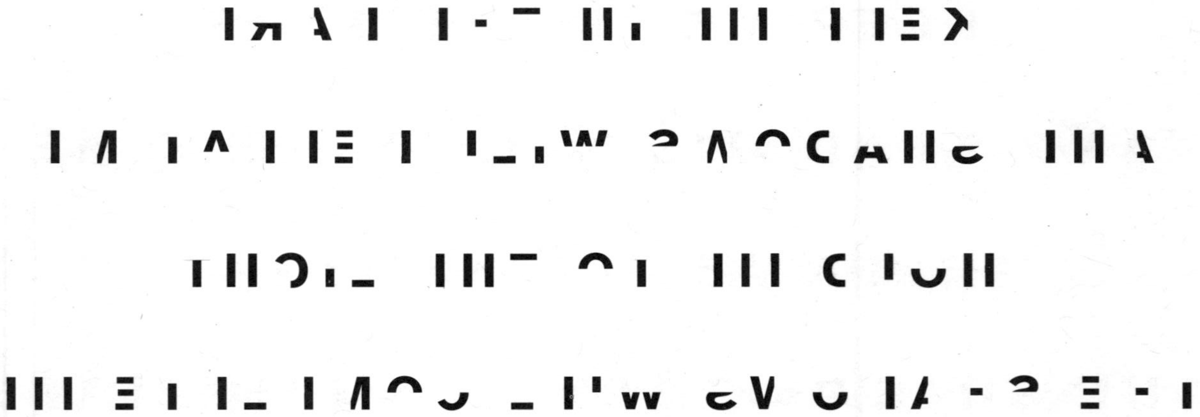

ACKNOWLEDGEMENTS AND NOTES

My greatest gratitude goes to Amy, Sophie, Ashey and Joseph, for bringing me back to life again and again.

Thanks, as always, to the high expectations and tireless exactations of Beth Follett. Thank you to Zab for her (as always) brilliant suggestions and design magic.

Grateful thanks to the Ontario Arts Council and to the Toronto Arts Council.

Michael Joseph, Lissa Paul and Lenore Look have all provided endless encouragement, as have my parents, Jim and Glen.

Thanks to James Pickersgill of POW! in Cobourg, ON, for first publishing "The Standoff Ends," as well as other poems of mine in *poetry'z own* over the past few years.

Steven Stratychuk, of Kitchener-Waterloo, was the twenty-one year old gunner of the tank captained by my great-uncle, Norman Allen. Stratychuk was killed when their tank was hit by a shell on February 26, 1945 near Goch in the Reichswald, Germany. As far as I know (I've tried to contact every Stratychuk in Canada) he has no living family. He's buried in Groesbeek Cemetery, The Netherlands. My great-uncle, badly injured at the same time, died of his wounds several years later.

"[T]he tongue in his cheek was dead" is taken from a line in one of my daughter Sophie's poems — her original line was "the tear on his cheek was dead."

"Hold me to the light" — the idea of how to do this came from an uncollected piece bpNichol once did called *AFTER WINSOR MCCAY*, grOnk, ZAP 2, Ganglia Press, 1983. Bearded bp bibliographer jwcurry showed it to me sometime around 1990 and I couldn't stop thinking about it.

"Chrysalis," commissioned by Ailbhe Darcy for www.moloch.ie, is in response to an art piece of the same name.

Thank you also to Anne Green, at Wordfest in Calgary, who provided an audience through which I could experiment with some of these pieces.

I'm grateful to Amalia Tomangong for all of her help at home.

Sophie Freedman-Lawson's *Collected Poems*, Ashey Freedman-Lawson's *Pensées Politiques* and Joseph Freedman-Lawson's *Talking Without Esses*, are all books that exist in the future. I urge everyone to find their way there.

Thank you to Charles Fernyhough for permission to use a quote from his book, and to Adnan Ali for permission to quote the lines of his I've included. You might want to look at Ali's website "Kuch Sunao" which means (according to him) "'Tell me something' — it's what you say to a friend when you just want to hear their voice." Thank you to the incomparable Lenore Look, for allowing me to use a quote from *Alvin Ho*.

Thank you also to Norañjo Alsnow, poet laureate of Doggerland, for permission to quote from his *Canciones de la botella vacía.*

The title of the book is taken from the recent (2008) D.W. Goedhuys translation of Adriaen Van Der Donck's "A Description of New Netherland" (1655). It's one of the only early sources of information about the Mahicans (Muhhekunneuw — or "People of the River"), from whom I am, in part, descended. In a section on whether or not the Mahicans can be Christianized, Van Der Donck observes the following:

> "They do know something of God, as we shall remark later, and are in great fear of the devil, for he harms and torments them. When they have been out fishing or hunting, they customarily throw a portion of the catch into the fire without ceremony and say, "There, devil, you eat that."

When I read this it struck me that poetry, when it works, gives the devil in you something to chew on.

JonArno Lawson lives in Toronto, Ontario with his wife and three children. He is the author of several books of poetry for adults and children.